The Bill of Rights

by Norman Pearl

illustrated by Matthew Skeens

PICTURE WINDOW BOOKS
Minneapolis, Minnesota

Special thanks to our advisers for their expertise:

Melodie Andrews
Associate Professor of Early American and Women's History
Minnesota State University, Mankato

Susan Kesselring, M.A., Literacy Educator
Rosemount–Apple Valley–Eagan (Minnesota) School District

❧

Editor: Nick Healy
Designer: Abbey Fitzgerald
Page Production: Melissa Kes
Art Director: Nathan Gassman
Associate Managing Editor: Christianne Jones
The illustrations in this book were created digitally.

Picture Window Books
5115 Excelsior Boulevard, Suite 232
Minneapolis, MN 55416
877-845-8392
www.picturewindowbooks.com

Printed in the United States of America.

Library of Congress Cataloging-in-Publication Data
Pearl, Norman.
The Bill of Rights / By Norman Pearl ; Illustrated by Matthew Skeens.
p. cm. — (American symbols)
Includes bibliographical references and index.
ISBN-13: 978-1-4048-2213-9 (library binding)
ISBN-10: 1-4048-2213-5 (library binding)
ISBN-13: 978-1-4048-2219-1 (paperback)
ISBN-10: 1-4048-2219-4 (paperback)
1. United States. Constitution. 1st-10th Amendments—Juvenile
literature. 2. Constitutional amendments—Juvenile literature.
I. Title.
KF4750.Z9P43 2007
342.7303—dc22   2006027220

Table of Contents

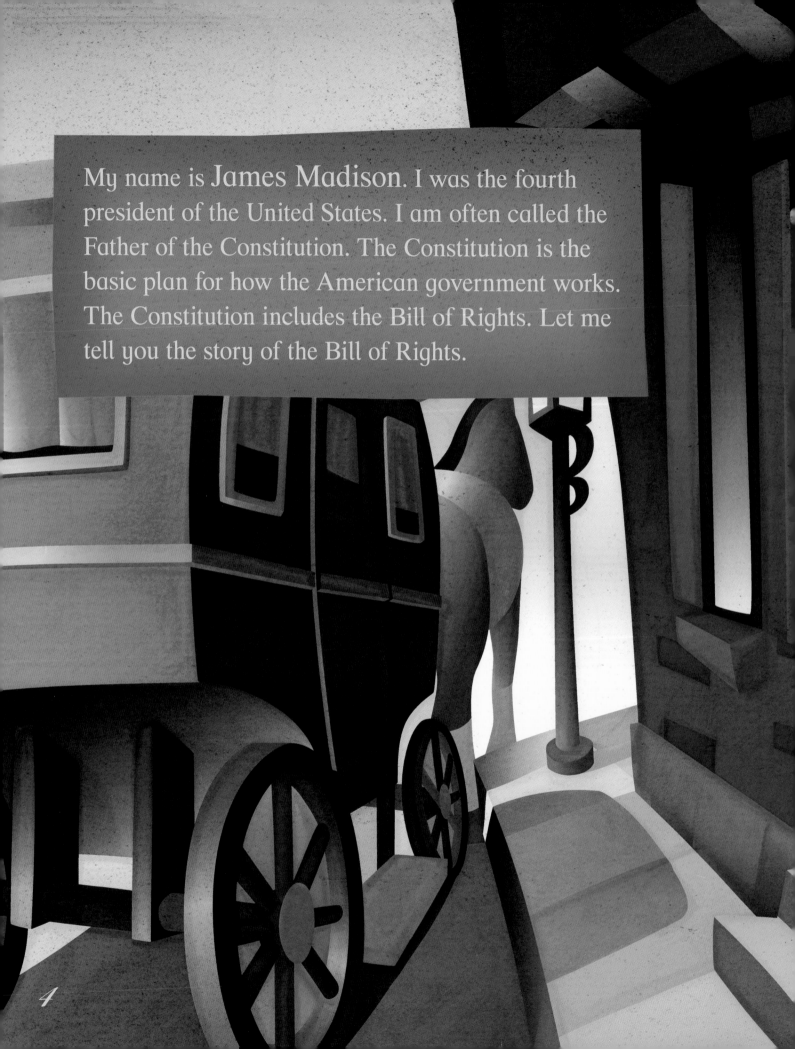

My name is James Madison. I was the fourth president of the United States. I am often called the Father of the Constitution. The Constitution is the basic plan for how the American government works. The Constitution includes the Bill of Rights. Let me tell you the story of the Bill of Rights.

What Is the Bill of Rights?

Americans love freedom. The country was created with the idea that people are born with certain rights, or freedoms. The Bill of Rights is a list of some of the most important rights.

The 1787 meeting in Philadelphia was called the Constitutional Convention.

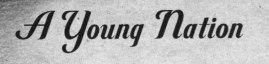

A Young Nation

In 1776, the American Colonies broke free of British rule. The Colonies set up a new government. Americans fought long and hard to win their freedom.

By 1787, many people were unhappy with the government that had been created for the new nation. Twelve of the 13 states sent delegates to Philadelphia, Pennsylvania, to work out a better plan.

A New Constitution

The states sent a total of 55 delegates to write the Constitution.
The group included George Washington, Benjamin Franklin,
and Alexander Hamilton. James Madison was a delegate
from Virginia.

The Constitution describes how the U.S. government is set up. It explains how laws are made and who makes them. It also describes the president's job and the role of the U.S. courts. But many leaders thought the Constitution should do more. They thought it should explain and guard the freedoms of the American people.

Writing the Bill of Rights

Some of the people who wrote the new Constitution wanted to make sure people's most important rights were protected. They later made a list of freedoms to add to the Constitution. This list became known as the Bill of Rights. It was a list of 10 amendments, or additions, to the Constitution.

The states had to accept the Bill of Rights before it was officially added to the Constitution.

Ten Important Amendments

The Bill of Rights includes the first 10 amendments to the Constitution. The rights it protects are still important to every American. No matter who is elected to office, these most basic freedoms remain.

The Bill of Rights was approved on December 15, 1791. Every December 15 is Bill of Rights Day in the United States.

First Amendment

The First Amendment protects the right to free speech and a free press. In the United States, people are free to say what they think. Newspapers do not have to be approved by the government. The First Amendment also allows people to hold meetings and to worship as they wish.

Second Amendment

The Second Amendment protects the right to bear arms.
This means people are free to own guns.

Third and Fourth Amendments

The Third and Fourth Amendments protect the right to privacy. The government cannot post soldiers in the homes of American people. Also, police cannot enter or search homes without a good reason.

Fifth to Tenth Amendments

The Fifth, Sixth, Seventh, and Eighth Amendments protect all people accused of crimes. These people have a right to a fair and speedy trial. They also cannot be punished in a cruel or unusual way.

The Ninth and Tenth Amendments explain that Americans have rights other than the ones listed in the Bill of Rights.

Freedom with Limits

Freedom is important to the way of life in the United States. But freedom has limits. Americans are not free to harm others or to take away others' rights.

For example, people cannot yell "Fire!" in a crowded movie theater if there is no fire. Doing so would be dangerous for other people. They might be hurt as they tried to rush out of the building.

Americans hope to balance each person's rights with the rights of others.

Seeing the Bill of Rights

You can see the Bill of Rights. It is in the National Archives building in Washington, D.C. The Bill of Rights is kept in a large case that is bombproof and bulletproof. The Constitution rests in the center of the case. On either side lie the Declaration of Independence and the Bill of Rights.

In 2003, a new display area opened at the National Archives, and that is where the Bill of Rights is today.

Armed guards watch over the case because these documents are so important to Americans. Like the other documents, the Bill of Rights is a symbol of freedom. The United States was built on the idea of freedom for all people.

Later Amendments

The Bill of Rights was a great start. However, as time passed, Americans saw that more freedoms needed protection. Over the years, more amendments have been added to the Constitution. Some of these later amendments helped give freedom to all Americans. For example, one amendment freed African-American slaves. Others made sure all men and women had the right to vote.

I hope you enjoyed the story of the Bill of Rights!

A total of 27 amendments have been added to the Constitution.

Bill of Rights Facts

❧ James Madison originally wanted 12 amendments added to the Constitution, but only 10 were approved.

❧ The National Archives, where the Bill of Rights is on display, holds more than 10 billion documents and 30 million photos. Nearly 3 million charts and maps are kept there, too.

❧ Adding an amendment to the Constitution is not easy. While just 27 amendments have been approved through the years, thousands of other amendments have been proposed.

❧ During World War II (1941–1945), the Bill of Rights was stored in a vault at Fort Knox, Kentucky. The government wanted to keep it safe in case the enemy attacked Washington, D.C.

Glossary

amendment — an addition or correction

archives — places where important papers from the past are kept

arms — guns

constitution — the written ideas and laws upon which a government is based

delegate — a person who is chosen to speak for others

document — a paper containing important information

national — belonging to a country

press — newspapers, magazines, and their writers

privacy — being alone or having to do with only one person

slave — a person who is owned by another person and is not free

symbol — an object that stands for something else

worship — to show a belief in God

To Learn More

At the Library

Hamilton, John. *The Bill of Rights.*
Edina, Minn.: Abdo, 2005.

Venezia, Mike. *James Madison.* New
York: Children's Press, 2004.

Yero, Judith. *The Bill of Rights.*
Washington, D.C.: National
Geographic, 2004.

On the Web

FactHound offers a safe, fun way to find
Web sites related to this book. All of the
sites on FactHound have been researched
by our staff.

1. Visit *www.facthound.com*

2. Type in this special code:
   1404822135

3. Click on the FETCH IT button.

Your trusty FactHound will fetch the best
sites for you!

Index

Look for all of the books in the American Symbols series:

The Bald Eagle
The Bill of Rights
The Great Seal of the
   United States

The Liberty Bell
Our American Flag
Our National Anthem
The Pledge of Allegiance

The Statue of Liberty
The U.S. Constitution
The White House